GRAND CANYON SUITE

Composed and scored

by

FERDE GROFÉ

EVANSTON PUBLIC LIBRARY
1703 ORRINGTON AVENUE
EVANSTON, ILLINOIS 60201

SUNRISE

It is early morning on the desert. The sun rises slowly spattering the darkness with rich colors of dawn. The sun comes from beyond the horizon and a brilliant spray of colors announces the full break of day.

The movement begins with a soft roll on the kettledrums, and a series of chords played by the woodwind follows. The main theme is played by the English horn. The development of the movement is taken up by other instruments reaching a triumphant climax that depicts the dawn of a new day.

THE PAINTED DESERT

The desert is silent and mysterious, yet beautiful. As the bright rays of the sun are reflected against majestic crags and spread across the sands in varying hues, the entire scene appears as a canvas thick with the pigments of nature's own blending.

The movement starts with a mysterious theme played by bass clarinet and viola accompanied by weird chords in the lower registers of the orchestra. It is interrupted by strange harmonies from the woodwind and the upper register of the piano. A contrasting melody of lyric quality follows. This is succeeded by the mysterious music which opened the movement.

ON THE TRAIL

A traveler and his burro are descending the trail. The sharp hoof beats of the animal form an unusual rhythmic background for the cowboy's song. The sounds of a waterfall tells them of a nearby oasis. A lone cabin is soon sighted and, as they near it, a music box is heard. The travelers stop at the cabin for refreshment. Now fully rested, the travelers journey forth at a livelier pace. The movement ends as man and burro disappear in the distance.

This is the most popular movement of the suite. It starts as the orchestra simulates the loud bray of a burro. After a violin cadenza, the first theme —a graceful melody in a rhythmic pattern—is established. It has the feeling of the burro walking. The second theme of the movement—a melody in Western style—is played contrapuntally to the first. This is followed by a suggestion of an old music box, which is played by the celeste. The opening theme is heard again in a faster tempo. The movement is concluded with the bray of the burro and the musical ending, itself, is short and incisive.

SUNSET

Now the shades of night sweep over the golden hues of day. As evening envelopes the desert in a cloak of darkness, there is a suggestion of animal calls coming from the distant rim of the canyon.

A wild, animal-like call, played by the horns, opens this movement. This is followed by the main theme, which is introduced by bells and violins. In the development, the theme is repeated by oboes and violins, then by woodwind and violins, again by cellos and horns, horns and flutes. Finally the horns again play the calls heard in the opening bars and the movement ends as the tones fade into the distance.

CLOUDBURST

This is the most pictorial movement of the suite. We hear the approach of the storm. Lightning flashes across the sky and thunder roars from the darkness. The torrent of rain reaches its height in a cloudburst, but the storm disappears rapidly and the moon comes from behind clouds. Nature again rejoices in all its grandeur.

Glissando effects in the violin section describe the approach of the storm. It is interesting to note how in the development of the movement Grofe uses all the resources of the orchestra to portray the battle of the elements. The agitated movement subsides, and then follows a gradual crescendo that reaches its climax at the very end.

GRAND CANYON SUITE

1. SUNRISE

Composed and Scored by
FERDE GROFÉ

Flutes I & II
Flute III & Piccolo
Oboes I & II
Eng. Horn
Bb Clars. I & II
Bass Clar.
Bassoons I & II
Contra Bassoon
I & II F Horns III & IV
I & II Bb Trumpets III
Trombs. I & II
Bass Tromb. & Tuba
Percussion
Bells & Chimes
Timp.
Celeste
Harp
Violin I
Violin II
Viola
Cello
Bass
SOLO
I
mf
pp
ppp

12

24

11 PRESTO

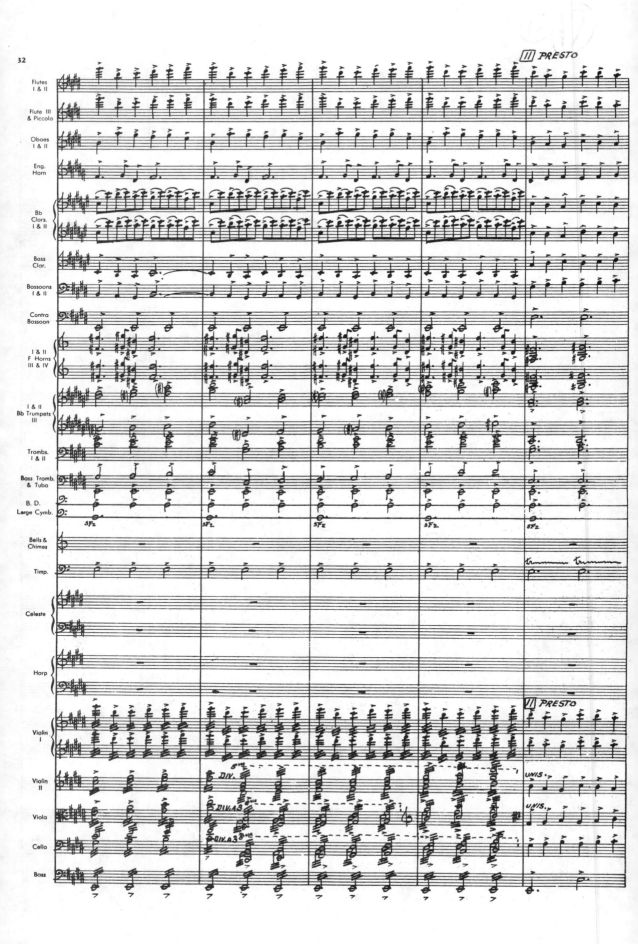

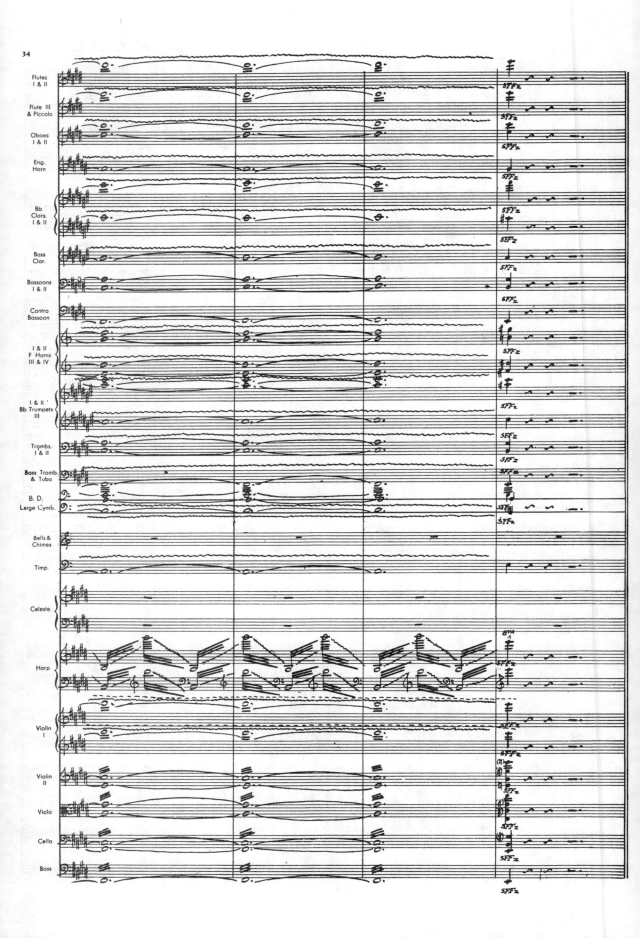

2. PAINTED DESERT

Composed and Scored by
FERDE GROFÉ

41

Flutes I & II
Flute III & Piccolo
Oboes I & II
Eng. Horn
SOLO
mf
mp
p
Bb Clars. I & II
pp
Bass Clar.
mp.
p
Bassoons I & II
pp
Contra Bassoon
pp
I & II F Horns III & IV
+
Fz
I & II Bb Trumpets III
Trombs. I & II
Bass Tromb. & Tuba
Percussion
Bells
VIBRAPHONE
Timp.
Piano
Harp
Violin I
Violin II
DIV.
Pizz.
pp
Viola
Cello
PIZZ
PP
Bass
PIZZ
PP

52

3. ON THE TRAIL

Composed and Scored by
FERDE GROFÉ

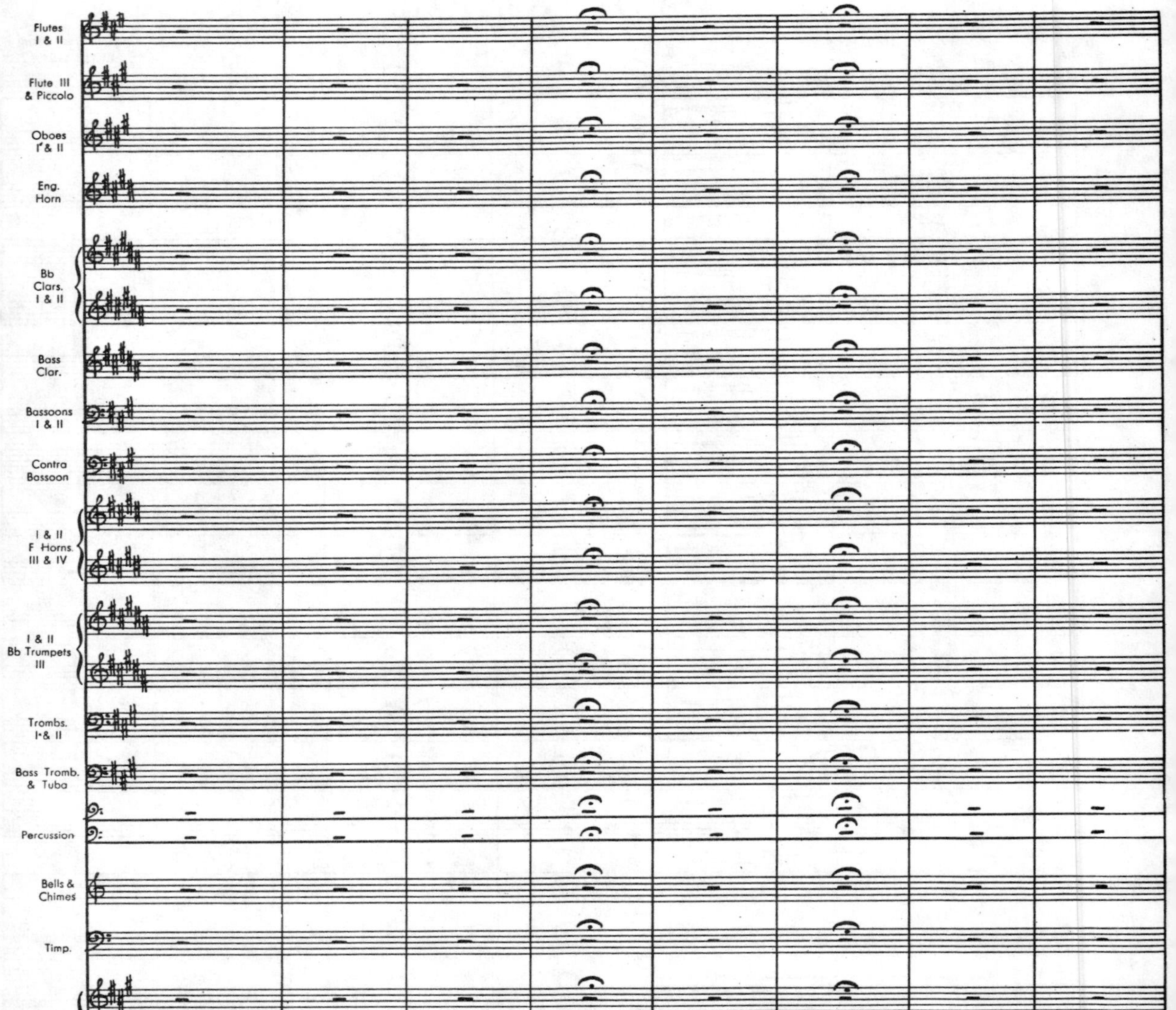

Flutes I & II
Flute III & Piccolo
Oboes I & II
Eng. Horn
Bb Clars. I & II
Bass Clar.
Bassoons I & II
Contra Bassoon
I & II F Horns III & IV
I & II Bb Trumpets III
Trombs. I & II
Bass Tromb. & Tuba
Percussion
Bells & Chimes
Timp.
Celeste
Harp
Violin I
Violin II
Viola
Cello
Bass
SUL G
MENO
mf

11 ALLEGRETTO POCO MOSSO (♩=72)

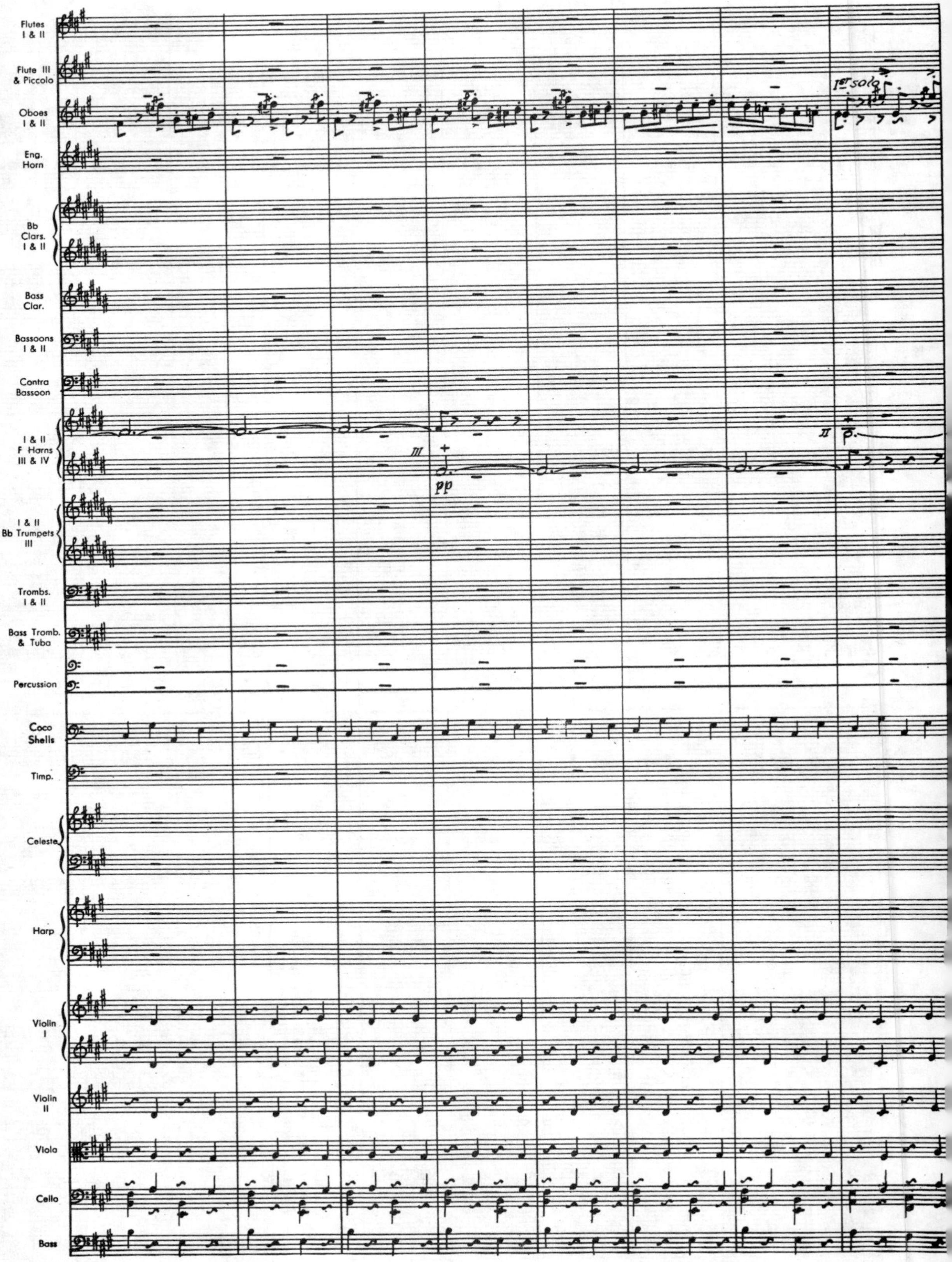

63

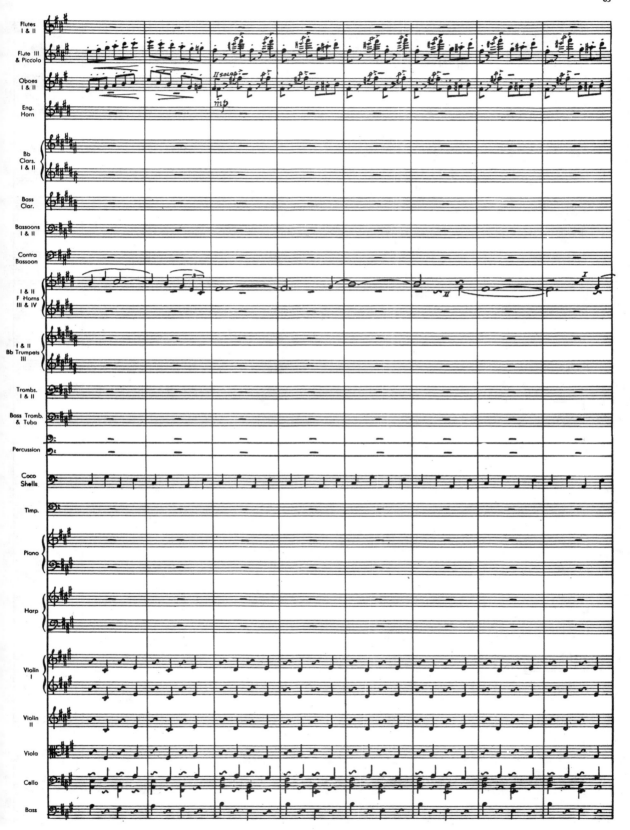

70

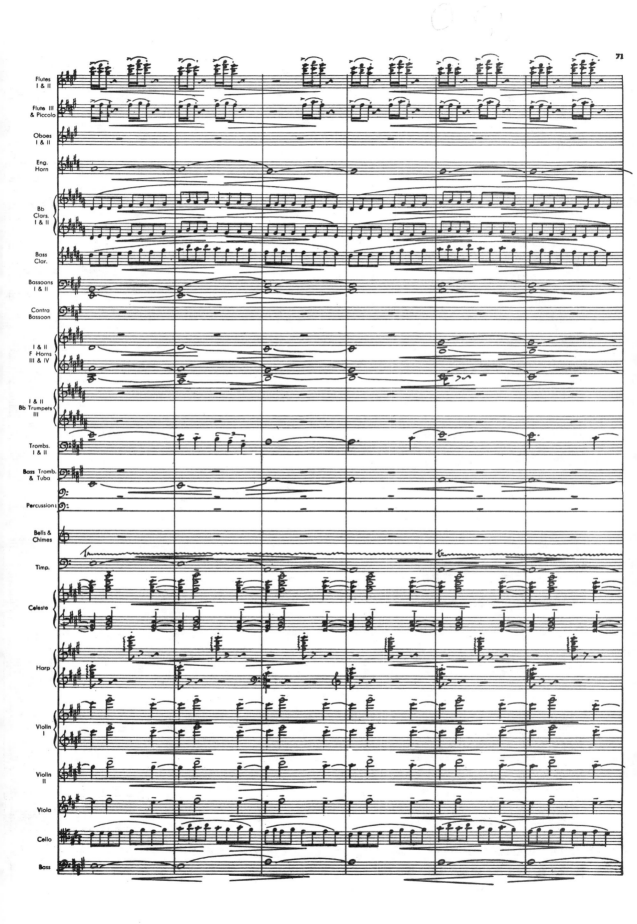

MODERATO

10 ANIMATO ♩.= 96

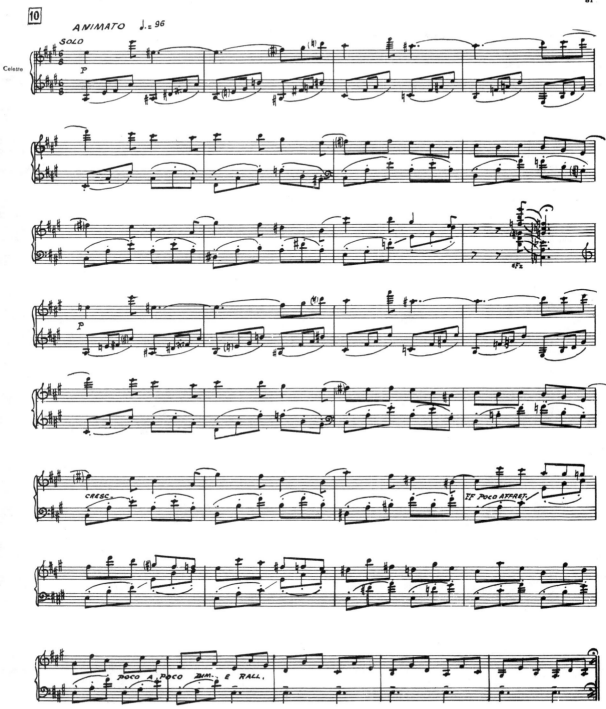

4. SUNSET

Composed and Scored by
FERDE GROFÉ

90

RUBATO
Flutes I & II
Flute III
Oboes I & II
Eng. Horn
Bb Clars. I & II
Bass Clar.
Bassoons I & II
Contra Bassoon
MUTED
I
mp
3
Fz
I & II F Horns III & IV
I
Fz
I & II Bb Trumpets III
Trombs. I & II
Bass Tromb. & Tuba
Triangle
Percussion
Bells
Timp.
Celeste
Harp
RUBATO
Violin I
Violin II
Viola
Cello
Bass

93

5. CLOUDBURST

Composed and Scored by
FERDE GROFÉ

115

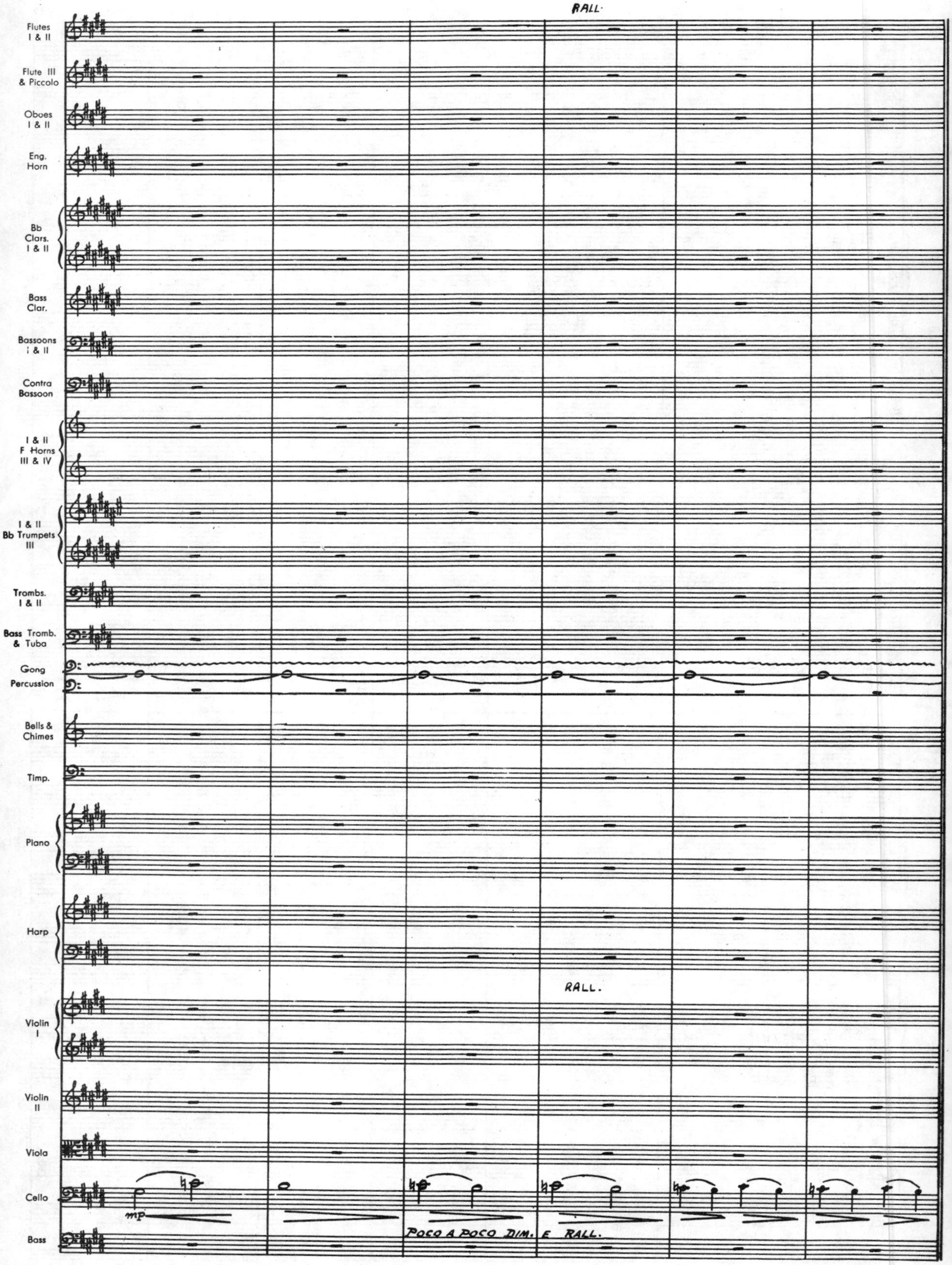
RALL.
Flutes I & II
Flute III & Piccolo
Oboes I & II
Eng. Horn
Bb Clars. I & II
Bass Clar.
Bassoons I & II
Contra Bassoon
I & II F Horns III & IV
I & II Bb Trumpets III
Trombs. I & II
Bass Tromb. & Tuba
Gong
Percussion
Bells & Chimes
Timp.
Piano
Harp
RALL.
Violin I
Violin II
Viola
Cello
mp
POCO A POCO DIM. E RALL.
Bass

5
Flutes I & II
Flute III & Piccolo
Oboes I & II
Eng. Horn
Bb Clars. I & II
Bass Clar.
Bassoon I
Bassoon II
I & II F Horns III & IV
I & II Bb Trumpets III
Trombs. I & II
Bass Tromb. & Tuba
Gong
Percussion
Bells & Chimes
Timp.
Piano
Harp
Violin I
Violin II
Viola
Cello
Bass
pp
pp
pp
III-IV
pp
5

120

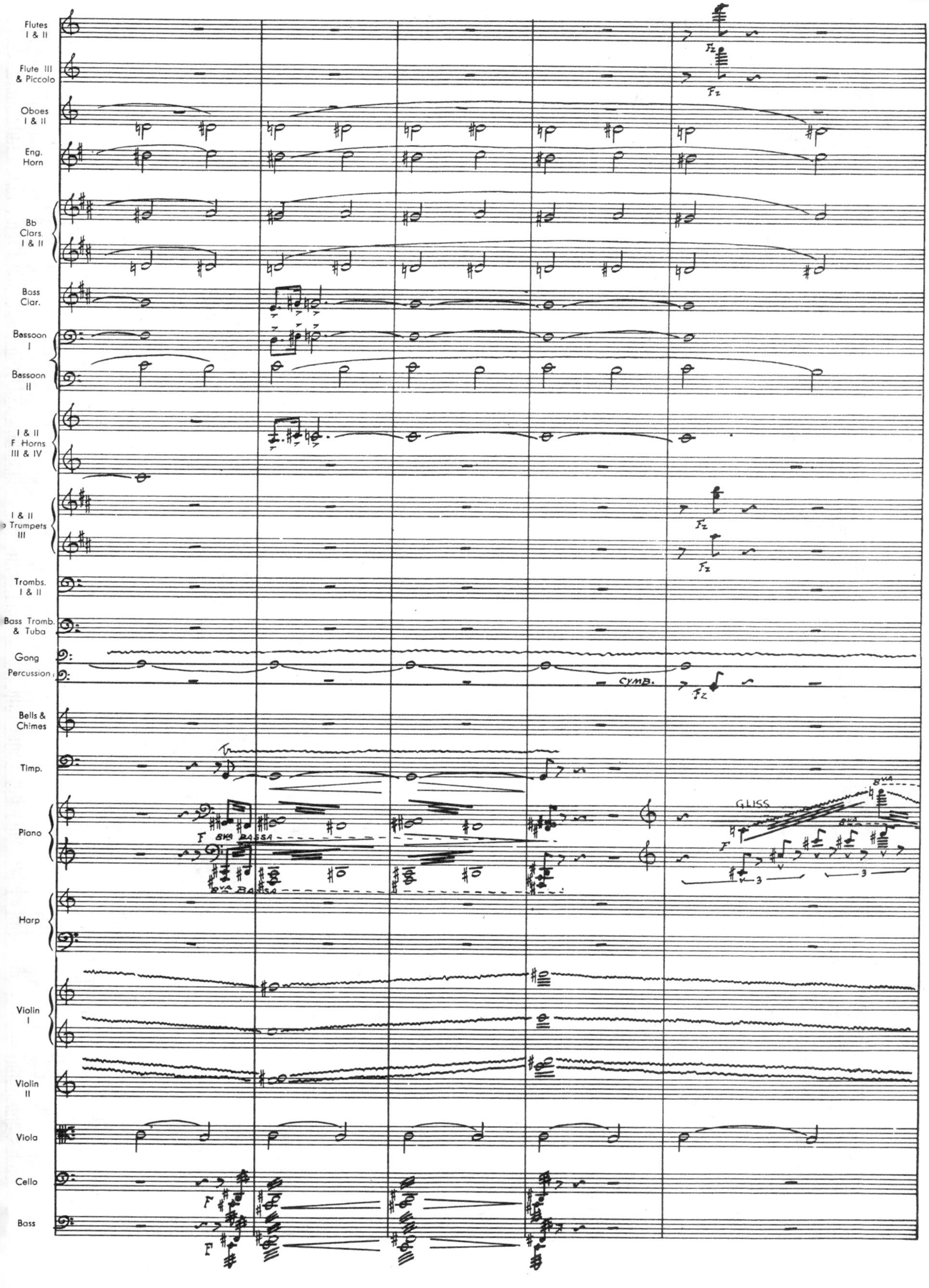

123

129

130

MOLTO CRESC.

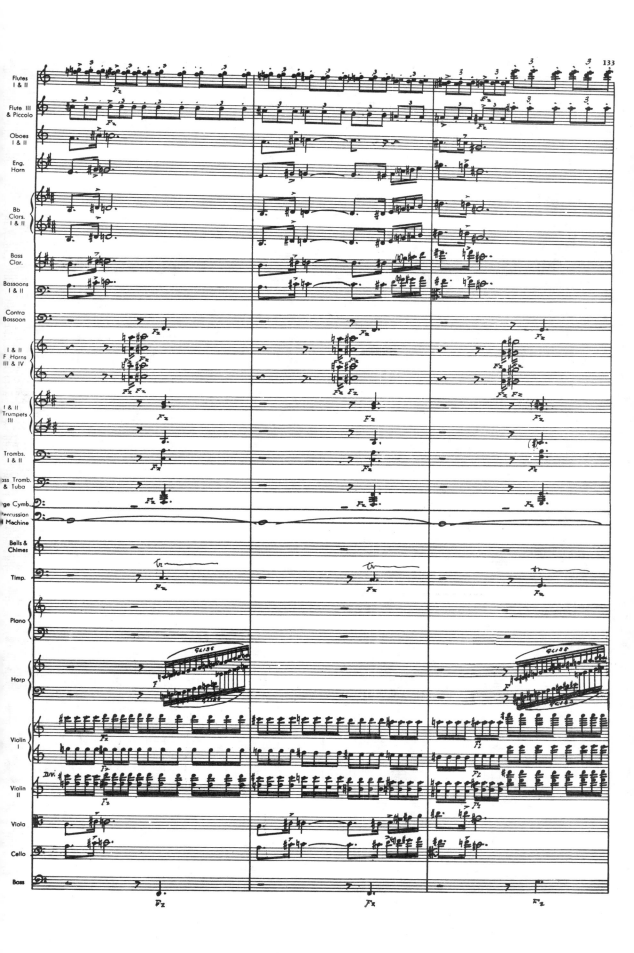

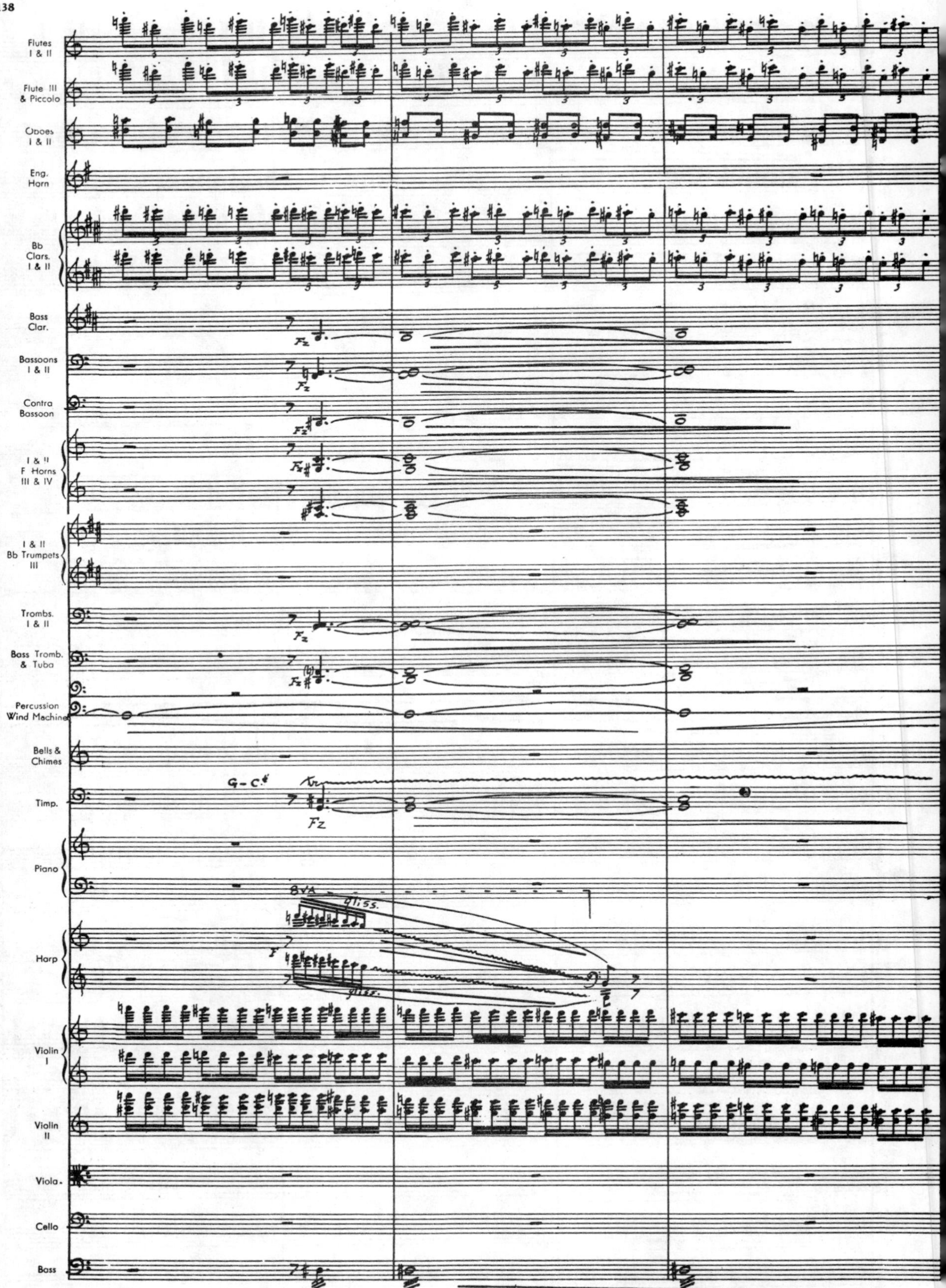

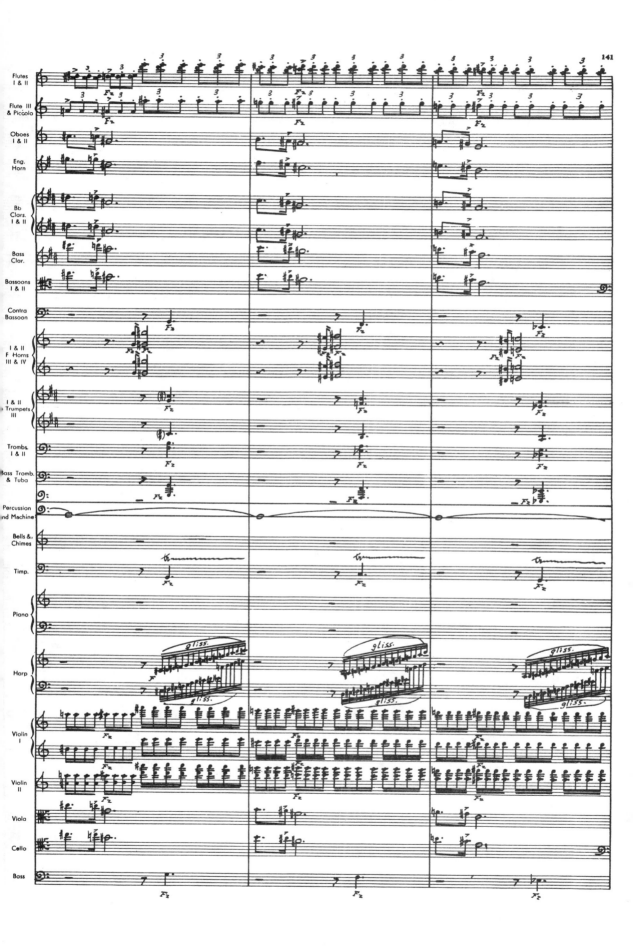

144

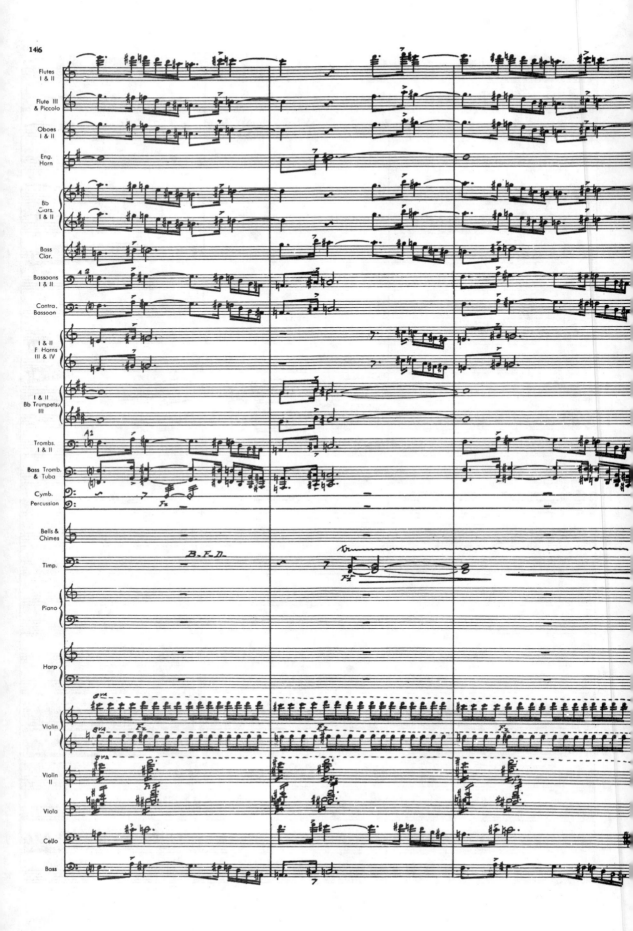

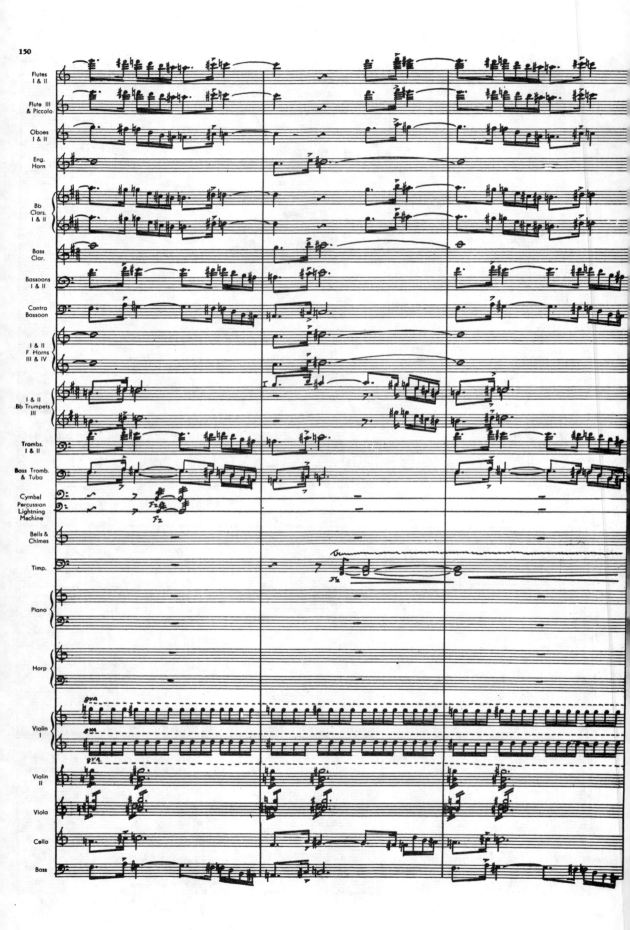

150

151

16
Flutes I & II
Flute III & Piccolo
Oboes I & II
Eng. Horn
Bb Clars. I & II
Bass Clar.
Bassoons I & II
Contra Bassoon
I & II F Horns III & IV
I & II Bb Trumpets III
HARD MUTE
Fz
HARD MUTE
Fz
Trombs. I & II
Bass Tromb. & Tuba
Cymb. Percussion
CYMBAL
Fz
Bells & Chimes
Timp.
Piano
PP
8va
Harp
16
Violin I
PP
PPP
Violin II
PP
PPP
Viola
Cello
Bass

lutes & II
ute III Piccolo
)boes & II
Eng. Horn
Bb Clars. I & II
Bass Clar.
assoons I & II
Contra assoon
I & II Horns II & IV
& II umpets III
rombs. I & II
ss Tromb. & Tuba
ercussion
Bells & Chimes
Timp.
Piano
Harp
Violin I
Violin II
Viola
Cello
Bass
mf
8va BASSA

Flutes I & II
Flute III & Piccolo
Oboes I & II
Eng. Horn
Bb Clars. I & II
Bass Clar.
Bassoons I & II
Contra Bassoon
I & II F Horns III & IV
a 2
I & II Bb Trumpets III
Trombs. I & II
Bass Tromb. & Tuba
Gong
Percussion
Bells & Chimes
F
Timp.
Piano
Harp
8va
Violin I
Violin II
Viola
Cello
Bass

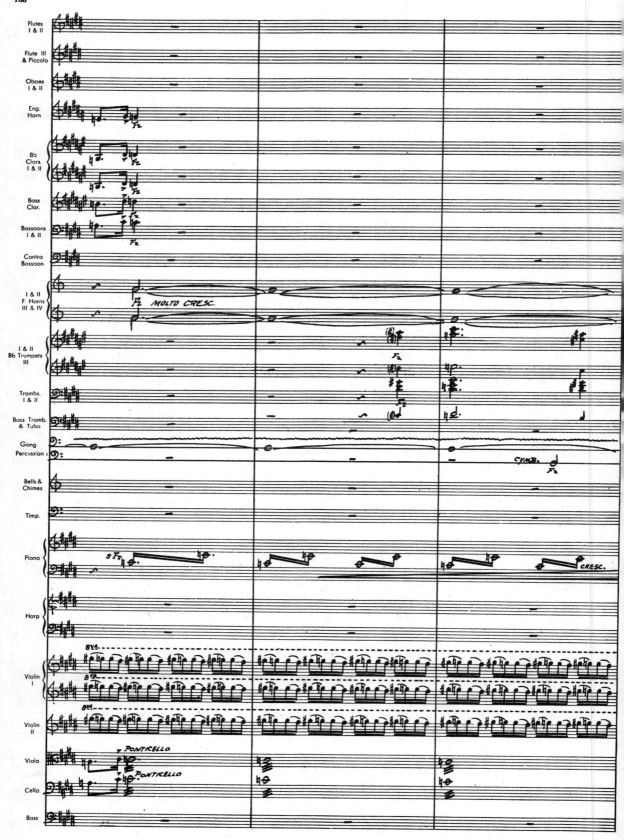

169

170